Farm Animals

Coloring Book

DP Kids

Bonus

Turn the page for bonus pages from some of our
most popular coloring and activity books.

Connect the Dots
Book for Kids

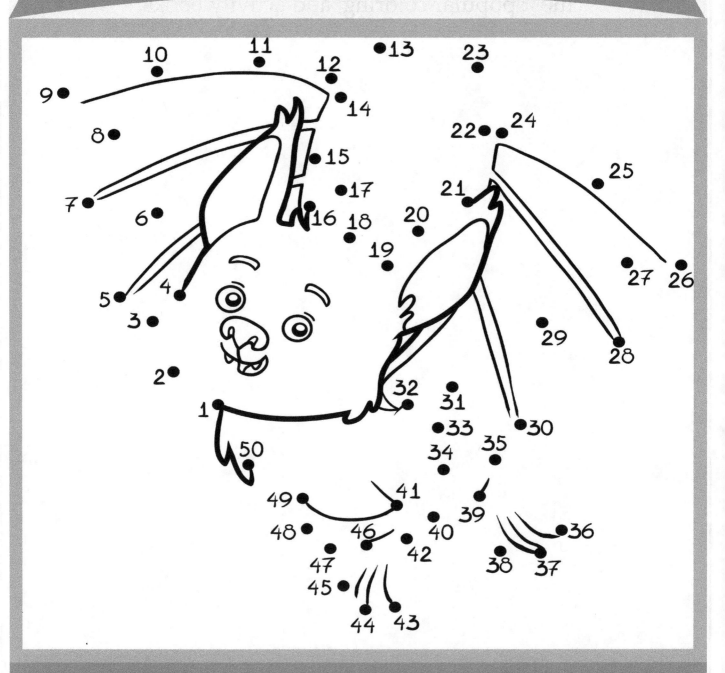

Challenging and Fun Dot to Dot Puzzles

DINOSAUR
COLORING BOOK FOR KIDS

DP KIDS

THINGS THAT GO
VEHICLE
COLORING
BOOK

CUTE CAT
COLORING BOOK

DP KIDS

Printed in the USA
CPSIA information can be obtained
at www.ICGtesting.com
LVHW011032021123
762858LV00043B/257

9 781947 243491